THE
MOST AWESOME

VIDEOS EVER!

First published in Great Britain in 2014 by Prion Books,
an imprint of the
Carlton Publishing Group
20 Mortimer Street
London W1T 3JW

A CIP catalogue for this book is available
from the British Library.

ISBN 978-1-85375-917-8

Project Editor: Matt Lowing
Editorial: Caroline Curtis and Conor Kilgallon

Printed and bound by CPI Group (UK) Ltd, Croydon CR0 4TY

10 9 8 7 6 5 4 3 2

THE
MOST AWESOME
YouTube
VIDEOS EVER!

150 of the coolest, craziest and funniest Internet clips

Adrian Besley

PRION

INTRODUCTION

Welcome to another amazing selection of the best videos available for free on YouTube. In a collection of awesome new and classic clips, you'll find plenty to make you laugh, leave you open-mouthed and maybe even bring a tear or two...

In February 2015, YouTube celebrates its 10th birthday. In a decade it has become an indispensable feature of the Internet and the most popular video-sharing site in the world. It is estimated that an hour of video is added to the site every second and around 100 million views are made every day.

Whatever you want to watch, you'll find it on YouTube: alongside countless music, sport and cat videos you'll find a never-ending supply of weird, hilarious, jaw-dropping, surreal and completely awesome clips.

This selection – including some of the most-watched videos ever and some relatively undiscovered gems – aims to reflect this variety. You can see the recent hits such as Miley Cyrus and Robin Thicke twerking, Chris Hadfield singing in space, the *Dumb Ways to Die* film and the brilliant BatDad as well as some YouTube classics, including Numa Numa, Fat Kid on Rollercoaster, Prancercise and Scared Boss. And, of course, there are side-splitting funnies, epic pranks, mind-boggling mash-ups, cute pets – and loads, loads more.

INAPPROPRIATE LANGUAGE WARNING

The videos selected do not contain any scenes of a sexual or extremely gross nature. However, there is the occasional use of mild bad language which is sometimes part of the video's humour. The comments sections of many of the clips often contain unnecessarily offensive, puerile and abusive language. They rarely feature any remarks of value and are generally worth ignoring completely.

DON'T TRY THIS AT HOME

Some of the book's clips feature stunts performed either by professionals or under the supervision of professionals. Accordingly, the publishers must insist that no one attempts to re-create or re-enact any stunt or activity performed on the featured videos.

HOW TO VIEW THE CLIPS

Each entry is accompanied by a QR code, which you can scan with your tablet or smart phone. Alternatively, there is a short URL address, which you can type into your own computer, tablet or phone. Unfortunately, many of the clips are preceded by adverts; these can often be skipped after a few seconds or you may wish to download a reputable advert blocker to prevent them appearing.

CONTENTS

"YouTube is a place for people to share their ideas.
If by people you mean 13-year-old girls and by ideas
you mean how they love the Jonas Brothers."

Bo Burnham

THE
MOST AWESOME
YouTube
VIDEOS EVER!

MY DAD'S A SUPERHERO

Nana, nana, nana, nana...

He's YouTube's very own superhero; a parenting vigilante, whose authentic-sounding, gravelly voiced diktats rule the roost in his family. When father of four Blake Wilson dons his Batman mask his family sit up and listen (OK, maybe his wife wears a slightly "not again" expression). Whether he's dishing out on table manners, dental hygiene, wearing safety belts or bedtime routines, it's performed with immaculate timing and great humour. Just one note of caution: anyone else get the feeling that his light-hearted warnings and rebukes might not go down quite so well once those kids become sullen, hypersensitive teenagers?

http://y2u.be/YlVi0noRr-o

BIEBER BUNNY BOILER

The rise and rise of the over-attached girlfriend

Not since the movie *Fatal Attraction* has a stalker made for such good entertainment. When Justin Bieber ran a competition for devoted female fans to submit "girlfriend" versions of his hit single "Boyfriend", Laina Walker grabbed her opportunity – but maybe not in the way Justin expected. Playing on the "needy" side of Bieber's song, Laina portrays an insanely jealous stalker-girlfriend brilliantly, with awesomely creepy intensity, incredible staring ability and hilarious lyrics. Laina has since become a YouTube celebrity, clocking up another hit with a "Call Me Maybe" parody and earning herself a major advertising contract.

http://y2u.be/Bqa-C4EbGqo

"A STUPID FOX SONG"

I think we all know what he says by now, thank you...

Norwegian comedy duo Ylvis claimed the top-trending video of
2013. Brothers Vegard and Bård Ylvisåker produced the video to
promote their TV series, but soon found themselves with a
global hit on their hands (paws?) as it took just 35 days to hit
100 million views. Even Bård called it "a stupid Fox song," but
damn it's catchy — acha-chacha-chacha-chow! Of course, it led
to hundreds of parodies, some better than others, with
perhaps the best being *What Does the Spleen Do?*
by Harvard Medical School students.

http://y2u.be/jofNR_WkoCE

UNICORNS OF THE SEA

Doner miss this whale of a tribute

It is about time YouTube took notice of the narwhal – the fabled unicorn of the sea. For far too long these majestic two-toothed inhabitants of Arctic waters have been uncelebrated on the web's prime site. OK, maybe Weebl, the producers of this catchy ditty, have gone a little over the top (are these whales really the Jedi of the sea?), and included some details David Attenborough might dispute (could they really beat a polar bear in a fight?), and are possibly just lying (did they really invent the shish kebab?), but the similarly unserenaded jelly fish would doubtless love to be honoured with such an awesome animation.

http://y2u.be/ykwqXuMPsoc

FREE YOUR INNER HORSE

Time to saddle up? Please say no – or should that be neigh?

Looking to get fit? Ready to get sweaty? Not afraid to look a complete idiot in front of the world? Then prancercise could be for you. This brand new dance/exercise, invented by Joanna Rohrback, mimics the movements of a horse – galloping, trotting and that strange head-bobbing thing. When the YouTube video went viral in 2013, many were left to ponder if this could be the new aerobics. Or were people just having a good laugh at a weird-looking woman who walks like there's something seriously wrong with her?

http://y2u.be/o-50GjySwew

McFLY ME TO THE MOON

Boybander Tom Fletcher sings his wedding speech

It's that part of the wedding everyone dreads. The groom stands, reaches for his notes and you brace yourself for an hour of excruciating boredom, endless thank-yous and having to laugh at feeble jokes. But not for the lucky guests at the wedding of McFly's Tom Fletcher. For Tom decided to sing his speech, changing the words of his band's greatest hits to pay tribute to his new wife, her parents, the ushers etc, etc, etc... Sounds dreadful? Gushing, pretentious and embarrassing? Well actually, it isn't. It's well-performed, perfectly judged and, go on, admit it, touching.

http://y2u.be/27WufdasQYs

FIRE, POLICE, AMBULANCE ... SIR ALEX FERGUSON?

Of course it's an emergency – United lost!

When is an emergency an emergency and when is it just an unfortunate and rather embarrassing situation? Many of us have experienced that dilemma. Is that my teenage son climbing into next door's window or an intruder? Can I ease the toddler's head out of the park railings or is oxyacetylene equipment needed? Do I have bubonic plague or is it just bad acne? Should I call the emergency services or not? On such occasions, this is the kind of bloke you want around. He doesn't demur. He doesn't dither. He's decisive. Manchester United, one of the world's biggest football teams, are having a mediocre season, so he calls 999.

http://y2u.be/2wjjvZeOazY

MAKING MILEY LOOK PANTS

Wrecking the wrecking ball

YouTube has no qualms about members posting the best of other social video networks, so increasingly we find videos crossing over from Vine, Vimeo and, in this case, Chatroulette. The amazing success of Miley Cyrus' videos provoked many parodies, but clad in Y-fronts and a vest, Steve Kardynal gives it his all. His split-screen Chatroulette followers watch in amazement, hilarity, disbelief and shock as bearded Steve dutifully hammers and writhes on his home-made wrecking ball. His spoof video received over nine million views in 24 hours, surpassing the views received by Miley's own performance of the song at the 2013 American Music Awards.

http://y2u.be/W6DmHGYy_xk

DAWG! LOOK AT HIM GO!

Tillman – the most famous dog on wheels

In 2009, Tillman the English bulldog set a world record for the fastest 100m canine skateboard, covering the distance in 19.678 seconds. These days, "Pot Roast", as he's nicknamed, is a celebrity dog. He's a TV star with his own Facebook page and it really would be no surprise to find him hanging around bus stops in baggy shorts and Vans. Tillman's talents and rise to fame are well chronicled on YouTube. Let's just hope he doesn't get hooked on chews, start paying for visits from bitches and begin endless visits to canine rehab.

http://y2u.be/DO3Awc2lo1k

DYING TO SEE YOU

The strangest – and best – ever safety warning

What kind of safety advice would recommend using your private parts as piranha bait? Only the funniest and most entertaining thing to come out of Australia since Harold Bishop left *Neighbours*. Those advertising folk can be pretty clever. Tasked to come up with a safety message to warn kids about fooling around near train tracks, the agency devised a multi-award-winning animation. It draws you in with a beautifully sung catchy ditty and a series of adorable, colourful cartoon blob characters, before hitting you with some gruesome – if amusing – words and images. Nothing short of YouTube genius.

http://y2u.be/IJNR2EpSOjw

JUST HOBBIT OF FUN

Elvishly yours...

Here's the choice. You could sit through 30 hours of *The Lord of the Rings* trilogy and follow the seemingly endless adventures of Benbo Bodkins and his merry band of leprechauns — or you could give up two minutes of your time to enjoy this piece of YouTube frippery. You'll get the beautiful scenery, Orlando Bloom, some endearing little creatures and a jolly tune to hum along to. No contest. And fair play to the lead man: seek out *Orlando Bloom "They're Taking the Hobbits to Isengard" Live* and see the film's star enjoying a laugh-along, sing-along version.

http://y2u.be/bZ2oWNsVt38

AWW! WE'VE STILL GOT IT!

Yep – a year on and humans are still awesome

Awesomeness? It's all relative, right? You might think
getting your history assignment in on time was a pretty good
achievement for the year, right? But British band Hadouken!
looked for something a little more exciting for the follow-up to
their 2012 viral video hit *People are Awesome*. To the soundtrack
of *Levitate*, one of the band's catchy indie pop songs, we get
some of the best of YouTube's jumpers, divers and somersaulters
– with the odd daredevil lunatic stunt thrown in here and there.
Fabulously edited and with real gobsmacking feats,
it's worth interrupting your homework to watch.

http://y2u.be/A6XUVjK9W4o

EXTREME WAKE-UP CALL

Ghostly goings-on in perfect prank

"I wanted to see how my girlfriend would react to a ghost coming out the TV trying to grab hold of her." Of course he did. It's not enough for James Williams to make scary noises from behind the sofa or jump out of the wardrobe as she goes to choose a dress. James really, really, really wants to frighten her out of her skin. So, replicating a scene from horror film *The Ring*, he builds a realistic, life-size, papier-mâché ghost. While his girlfriend is sleeping, James clamps it to the TV, before waking her with a ghostly howl... Amazingly, the couple are still together.

http://y2u.be/UEnyJxaxTp8

UNIVERSITY CHALLENGE!

The most inspirational speech ever!

Next time your teacher, boss, sports coach or parents try to motivate you with some carefully chosen and well-rehearsed words, just fire this up and show them how it should be done. Nicholas Selby, a student at Georgia Institute of Technology, took up the challenge of welcoming new students to the university in Atlanta and produced what some have called the most inspirational speech ever. He does make it sound a great place. Wonder what grades you need?

http://y2u.be/98nNpzE6gls

CALL AND (NO) RESPONSE

Boom, boom, boom — everybody say... huh?

Hey guys, remember the Outthere Brothers? No? "Boom, Boom, Boom"? Still nothing? Well, never mind, it was a UK hit in 1995 and had a funky beat and a shout-out chorus. They say, "Let me hear you say 'way-ho'." You say, "Way-ho." Somehow, this song became quite a YouTube anthem. Norwegian teenager Catherine Marjorie Solumsmo clocked up most hits with her somewhat understated version on *CathyMay15 Boom Boom Boom Way Ho Girl*. But this is more fun, as Stuart Moffat tests out just who does remember the legendary ditty. Not many, then...

http://y2u.be/FuleTVQ5EoY

3D OR NOT 3D

Introducing the anamorphic optical illusion

This'll freak you out, but in an intriguing, mind-bending, nice way. We're talking anamorphic optical illusions here, which means that at one particular angle an image appears to be three-dimensional, but move your position and the whole thing distorts and changes. It's dead clever but basically an ancient art trick practised by the likes of Michaelangelo. Brasspup films some perfect examples using household items such as Rubik's Cubes and trainers. He even gives you links to print them out and try them yourself. Watch out for that cat, though!

http://y2u.be/tBNHPk-Lnkk

MARCHING POWER

Better than a half-time pie and a Bovril

If you think that pimply faced teenagers walking up and down playing trombones and drums at half-time is boring, take a look at this mob. Their Disney Tribute show was pretty impressive and their Video Games performance was gobsmacking, but then they took it up a level. Their Hollywood Blockbusters show, featuring tunes from *Superman, Lord of the Rings, Harry Potter, Jurassic Park* and *Pirates of the Caribbean*, is an awesome display of creative, er, marching up and down. Their performances really are impressive they're not nicknamed "The Best Damn Band in the Land" for nothing.

http://y2u.be/DNe0ZUD19EE

MARRIED BLISS

A gorgeous nurse turns out to be his wife

Ready for a little heart-warming gooeyness? And this time there's not a cat, dog or animated creature in sight. Meet Jason Mortensen. He's coming round after a hernia operation and is still feeling a little groggy. Fortunately, a nurse is on hand to check he's OK and feed him a cracker. More fortunate still, she has the foresight to film the unfolding events. That's because the "nurse" is about to reveal to Jason that she is actually his wife. How does he react? Get the tissues ready!

http://y2u.be/IqebEymqFS8

KILLER TIME

Do you have a question for a cold-blooded assassin?

What do you know about ninja? You may be aware that they
wear headbands, practise lethal martial arts and are deadly
assassins. Those who have studied them might tell you they
can be killed only by another ninja and that they can scale walls
effortlessly. But what if you need to know more? Look no further
than YouTube's *Ask a Ninja*. Here you can discover if ninjas catch
colds, what gift to give a ninja and how to play niniature golf.
But be careful out there. Don't get too near the screen —
behind each answer is a ninja just looking for a killing.

http://y2u.be/qdS5lkeN8_8

QUITE LITERALLY BEAUTIFUL

Music video that tells it like it is

YouTube's "literal" craze has produced some witty and clever videos. You may already have seen the A-ha "Take on Me" literal, where the lyrics are changed to reflect what actually happens in the video. In James Blunt's "You're Beautiful", James gets cold in the rain and that's about it, but we're treated to great lines like, "Now you're going to see my chest". If you're hooked on literals, you could also check out "Never Going to Give You Up" by the web's favourite figure of fun, Rick Astley.

http://y2u.be/YOII5Qiq-9g

TIME TRAVEL

Take a trip through the streets of London – past and present

Cinematographer Claude Friese-Greene's celebrated film *The Open Road* is a series of silent travelogues of Britain made to promote his late father's pioneering colour film process. In 1927 he completed filming the streets of London, capturing some fabulous images of the city. Now for the clever bit: in 2013 filmmaker Simon Smith followed his footsteps, filming exactly the same streets of the capital. How much has changed in the intervening 86 years? You might be surprised.

http://y2u.be/N8IXzSCOFZQ

ETCH-A-SKETCH

The animated comedy kings of YouTube

YouTube really is a world of its own and ASDF (Ass-Duff-Moo-Vee) are aristocracy. This series of simple but very funny cartoon animations by TomSka have notched up an amazing 100 million hits. Clever, random and zany, each video is made up of a number of sketches played out in distinctive line drawings, each lasting about 10 seconds. There's a pretty high hit-to-miss ratio of gags, visual jokes and slapstick, and the one-liners can be fabulous, but watch out — you won't be the only one repeating them in the office or playground.

http://y2u.be/CU0vWXKetec

TUBE TRAINING

Moscow subway squats

As if travelling by tube train isn't already enough of an assault
course – fighting for a space on the platform, jostling for elbow
room in the carriage and climbing hundreds of steps because the
escalator is broken – the Moscow system offered passengers the
choice of doing 30 squats in order to get a free ticket. Of course,
you can choose to pay for your ticket and avoid the humiliation
of getting on the train red-faced, sweaty and out of breath.
What do you mean, you look like that anyway?

http://y2u.be/qaPNDbGKr7k

HE SAID WHAT?!

What the stars of American football are talking about

The Bad Lip Reading channel really took off during the 2012
US Presidential Election campaign, when its sometimes
hilarious, sometimes bizarre, but always incorrect lip-reading
interpretations went viral. But the anonymous genius who puts
these together surpassed him- or herself with this fabulous
collection of American football heroes and their misquotes.
Look out for the Orange Peanut... classic.

http://y2u.be/Zce-QT7MGSE

WHEN IN ROME...

Three tenors for the price of one

It was the eve of the 1990 FIFA World Cup Final in Rome. With Britain still coping with the trauma of Gazza's tears at going out in the semi-final, the three greatest singers on the planet took to the stage to wring out the last bit of emotion left in the country. José Carreras, Luciano Pavarotti and Plácido Domingo (Homer Simpson's "third favourite" of the Three Tenors) came together in the ruins of ancient Rome to perform. Such was the reaction that the recording became the best-selling classical record ever and "Nessun Dorma" became a somewhat unlikely football anthem.

http://y2u.be/r8MbJAU8hDohttp

HELL NO!

Quiet night in

If you're one of those horror-movie watchers who constantly screams, "Why on earth would he go in there?" or "Why don't you just call the cops?" or even "Why a remote cabin in a dark wood? What's wrong with the Travelodge?", then *Hell No! The Sensible Horror Movie* is for you. Here are horror-film trailers where the characters make the right decisions. No gore, no goose bumps and certainly no flesh-eating zombies, just a lot of common sense.

http://y2u.be/Sq9m9u7loxM

THROWING THE BIG ONE

It's not fair! It's the greatest temper tantrum ever!

Your little brother thinks he's making a point as he slams the door and shouts, "I wish I'd never been born," then storms off to his bedroom to sulk. But he's got a fair way to go before he's even in the same league as Stephen Quire. Admittedly the teenager has been viciously provoked. His mum has just cancelled his World of Warcraft account. Who wouldn't fly off the handle? Unfortunately, he also has a cruel elder brother who's set up to film the whole thing – the threats to run away, the hyperventilating and that strange thing with the remote.

http://y2u.be/YerslyzsOpc

SOME CAFFEINE BUZZ!

The telekinetic coffee shop surprise

The corporate promotional prank race continues to evolve and the videos get ever more elaborate. This stunning stunt for the remake of the horror classic *Carrie* sets the bar pretty high. Over 50 million people have clicked on to watch the fall-out when a teenage girl freaks out over her flat white getting knocked over. We've already seen the preparation for the stunt, but the expression on the faces of the unsuspecting customers at a New York City coffee shop as the girl unleashes her "telekinetic powers" is utterly priceless. Just a shame that the movie turned out to be such a farmyard turkey!

http://y2u.be/VlOxlSOr3_M

UNLEASH YOUR INNER BABY

Mini-me mirror dancing

Evian's roller-skating babies ad set the record for the most-viewed online advertisement (over 170 million views) in 2009, so they needed to follow it up with something pretty special. Did they manage it? Well, they stuck to the same formula, found another nostalgia dance hit (Ini Kamoze's "Here Comes the Hotstepper") and brought in some dancing babies, this time mirror dancing to their lookalike adult selves. Quite what the whole thing has to do with bottled water is anyone's guess, but there's no doubt they've found themselves another hit — you'll watch it again and again.

http://y2u.be/pfxB5ut-KTs

TAKING THE RAP

It's the contest of the century: Mozart versus Skrillex

Nice Peter and Lloyd Ahlquist's hilarious rap battles have carved out a well-deserved niche in the YouTube community. Their boasting and insulting-in-rhyme competitions pit celebrities and historical and fictional figures against each other in two-minute bouts. Witty, imaginative and funny, they have become increasingly well produced since the early battles, such as Darth Vader versus Adolf Hitler. Other classic matches pit Mario Bros up against the Wright Bros and find Genghis Khan scrapping it out with the Easter Bunny, but this has to be a favourite if only for the classic line, "I've seen more complexity in a couch from Ikea."

http://y2u.be/_6Au0xCg3P!

CHOLESTEROL DAMAGE

Everything you shouldn't eat – in one epic meal

You've had your five-a-day fruit, a small salad and downed your ginseng yin-yang juice, but still feel a little peckish?

How about a recipe from the Epic Meal Time boys? These bacon-loving Canadian 20-somethings have gained notoriety concocting feasts that will have your arteries shrieking in fear. One-time substitute teacher Harley Morenstein and his gang use ingredients as diverse as waffles, cake mix, tortilla chips, maple syrup, fast food items, Baileys, cheese sticks and pounds and pounds of bacon. Their fast food pizza notched up 286g (10oz) of fat and 5,210 calories, but this gourmet delight exceeds even that!

http://y2u.be/jXjxHQQxcLw

HIT THE GROUND RUNNING

The incredible fate of the skydiving camera

A skydiver's helmet-mounted camera comes loose and falls out of the plane just as the diver is ready to jump. The camera drops all the way to the ground and, putting it down to bad luck, the diver gets on with his adrenaline-pumping life. Fast-forward eight months and a farmer comes across a camera. When he checks out the contents of its memory, he is amazed... and so will you be. This extraordinary accidental video captures the camera's spinning adventure and even has its own fabulous and surprising ending.

http://y2u.be/QrxPuk0JefA

MOVIE STAR CEREAL KILLER

Ryan Gosling won't eat his breakfast

If you want to create a successful Internet meme, your best bet is to hit on Hollywood star Ryan Gosling. The Internet just loves any Gosling-based fun. *Hey Girl* saw sultry Ryan uttering nauseating pick-up lines, *Feminist Ryan Gosling* gave his pronouncements a political bent and in *Ryan Gosling Breaks Up a Fight in New York* he does just that – what a hero! But there's something about Ryan refusing his cereal that tops the lot. Producer Ryan McHenry offers up spoonfuls of cornflakes at moments of intense drama and elicits some – unintentional – hilarious responses from the hunky actor.

http://y2u.be/jxs791pjOeg

CLASSROOM DROP-OFF

Detention for the drowsy duckling?

This is a situation that will have most of us sympathizing. You've had a tough morning followed by a nice lunch and are just about ready for a little afternoon nap. Then the bell goes and you're due back in the classroom. It doesn't matter how scintillating your teacher is, that dozy feeling just won't go away. So, here we are in an Australian college, listening to a lesson in accountancy and one poor chap – OK, it's the cutest of ducklings – just can't seem to stay awake. And trying to get up and leave proves an even worse idea. Just cuter than cute!

http://y2u.be/LGrpsZ7BsQA

WHOSE BED IS IT ANYWAY?

Who said anything about letting sleeping cats lie?

Since the great Treaty of Barking in the late 20th century, cats and dogs have maintained a reasonably harmonious relationship in domestic households around the world. But word is creeping out that the feline side is taking advantage of the non-aggression pact. This smuggled-out collection of videos is intended to alert the world's dogs to the bitter struggle being enacted. While the cats are by turn proud, smug, unabashed and downright inflammatory, the canines are singularly frustrated and powerless. "They're taking our beds now," they complain. "How much provocation do we have to take?"

http://y2u.be/Dod2VzUFNW0

HIGH-HANDED ARREST

The most eloquent and gentlemanly drunkard ever

Filmed in 1988, but a recent arrival on YouTube, this gem stars former chef Paul Charles Dozsa being shoved into a police car after pulling his "dine and dash" trick: ordering an expensive meal at a hotel, tucking in, then claiming he can't afford to pay. But Dozsa steals the show by being the most eloquent and gentlemanly drunkard ever to be manhandled (and he really is *man*handled) by the boys in blue. His outrage, protestations and language went viral and can't fail to raise a smile — even if you've seen it before.

http://y2u.be/pEsZkTTgydc

PIGLETMOBILE

Whee! Whee! Whee! All the way home

This little piggy was dropped off at a vet's in Florida, the owner expecting his cute little porker to be put down. For the little piglet, just 10 days old and weighing only 450g (1lb), had been born without the use of his hind legs. However, the vet, Len Lucero, had other ideas. Using a kid's construction toy, he set about building a wheelchair for the winsome little grunter, whom he named Chris P. Bacon. Chris seems to have taken to his mobility vehicle and you could say he's as happy as a pig on wheels!

http://y2u.be/4Z-uO5TPQfM

OLD DOG, NEW TRICKS

He's not called Jumpy for nothing...

This four-and-a-half-year-old border collie could just be the most talented mutt in the world. OK, he does the expected – the back-flipping Frisbee-catching, the surfing, the skateboarding and the slalom-running – but Jumpy has a whole host in his repertoire, some of them simply incredible. Just watch him go! And he can do charming, too. Indeed, with a wink and a modest paw over his face, Jumpy appears to be a better actor than many of his human Hollywood counterparts. Want to see more of Jumpy? Search for *Bad Ass Dog 2+*.

http://y2u.be/5I_QzPLEjM4

SQUEAK UP LITTLE GUY

The most adorable frog in the world

It had to happen eventually. For years, YouTube has bombarded us with adorable kitties, bewitching mutts, sneezing pandas and dramatic chipmunks, but now an amphibian has joined the parade – and what a little cutie it is, too. This is a desert rain frog but it actually resembles a plastic dog-chew toy. It even makes an endearing squeak, which we are informed is its "war cry". However, don't be deceived – this brutal killer can leap up to 2.5m (8ft) and take your ear off with a single bite. Just kidding! Awwww! Look at its little sandy rump.

http://y2u.be/cBkWhkAZ9ds

EASTLEIGH'S GOT TALENT

Do the bus stop shuffle

It's even worse than George Orwell predicted in *1984*. Not only is our every move being monitored by CCTV cameras, but now everyone is a talent spotter and we're all auditioning. There was a time when you could pick your nose, scratch your backside or adjust your pants in public. But no longer. Take Ellie Cole from Eastleigh, Hampshire. She was just waiting for a bus and bopping along to Alesha Dixon's "Knock Down" on her headphones. The next thing she knows, she's gone viral as the Dancing Queen of the Bus Stop. Heaven help us all!

http://y2u.be/I0mmVPV4w7c

FATHER'S DAY

Schoolboy's day of reckoning

We'll leave this one to Aria Shahrokhshahi, the lad who set up a camera to film his dad's reaction to his news: "Hey there, everyone, the man in the video is my dad. One year before this video I was a grade F in maths and in England you need a C (pass) to basically do anything with your life. I've never been amazing academically and have struggled throughout school..."
If you want to see the opposite reaction, find *Irish Father's Priceless Reaction After Son Pretends to Fail*.

http://y2u.be/Ls9Cg8iaq1s

MATCH OF THE DAY

Strike a light! It's a slow-mo match head

You strike a match. It ignites and burns, until you do that panicky shaking thing when your fingers get too hot. That's about it for most of us, but by shooting a match head at 4,000 frames per second, the Ultra-Slo Studio team reveal the whole process in amazing detail. Taking a couple of minutes to even get to the flame, we see, in super-close-up, the chemical reaction that results in fire. Even if you're not interested in the science, it's a bewitching couple of minutes' viewing.

http://y2u.be/_074G_bk5sY

MAXIMUM DPH (DUMBNESS PER HOUR)

Because there's maths, applied maths, pure maths and plain wrong maths

---

On a road trip to Boise, Idaho, Travis Chambers asked his wife Chelsea a simple maths question: if you're travelling at 80 miles per hour, how long does it take you to go 80 miles? She tried to work it out in her head, he posted her four-minute response, and soon it was registering millions of hits. As her complex calculations went viral, Travis even left a comment: "This is not going to be easy to break to my wife." Just how long does it take a humiliated spouse to throw a tablet across a room, then?

http://y2u.be/Qhm7-LEBznk

TRICK AND TREAT

The amazing Halloween stick kid

Ah, those scary Halloween kids. They come knocking at your door with greased back hair and some plastic fangs and you're expected to dish out fistfuls of Haribos. But if you met Zoe down a dark alley, I bet your heart would miss a beat or two. Zoe's dad, Royce Hutain of Huntington Beach, California, made the toddler an LED suit, transforming her into a ghostly walking stick figure. Cute and scary in one outfit — you can just guess how brimful her little bucket was that night.

http://y2u.be/GkBDRUO8hAo

EXTREME PREJUDICE

Some of my best friends are...

Fortunately racism rarely rears its ugly head on YouTube, but hopefully on this occasion you'll forgive its appearance because this video is very, very funny. The news reporter, it seems, is on the trail of a highly controversial story. An Aussie householder has placed a classified ad announcing the sale of his house with the stipulation, "No Asians". The reporter and his news crew manage to corner him in front of the property, determined to hold him to account. His explanation isn't exactly what they expected...

http://y2u.be/0YM9Ereg2Zo

HAPPY FEET

Street soccer flicks and tricks bring Internet hits

When you were a kid you might have called it "keepie-uppie", but they've now made a sport of it and it's known as "freestyle football". It's actually a collection of incredibly skilful and jaw-dropping moves – think of a show-off version of Cristiano Ronaldo (OK, maybe that doesn't work). Anyway, meet Arnaud "Séan" Garnier and his incredible array of fancy footwork. He demonstrates his art amid some busy crowds but you can't help wondering how he'd fare against a hefty centre-back clogger on a wet night in Grimsby.

http://y2u.be/yxQHgVhxfMc

CAN'T TASE THIS!

Student in most embarrassing stun gun appeal ever

This clip, taken from a dull 2007 speech by US Senator
John Kerry at the University of Florida, launched a phrase
that has appeared in songs, TV episodes, ring tones and on
T-shirts. It's not the dreary Kerry who says it, though, but earnest
student Andrew Meyer, who found out that only senators
can get away with being truly dull. As his own stultifying
contribution to the debate is met by police wielding their
favourite toy gun, Meyer shrieks his homeboy plea. It
didn't take long for YouTubers to work their magic.

http://y2u.be/QkkLUP-gm4Q

SPLIT PERSONALITY

Jean-Claude in epic truck-to-truck stunt

Two trucks, the Muscles from Brussels and an awesome sunset was all it took (in just one take, according to the producers) to send this Volvo ad into the viral stratosphere. Whether or not you take in the whole "pair of legs engineered to defy the laws of physics" spiel or the Volvo precision steering message, it's a pretty impressive 90 seconds' work. Of course, these hard men being what they are, it wasn't long before it was challenged. Chuck Norris, indeed, produced a pretty funny parody in *Greetings From Chuck Norris (the Epic Christmas Split)*.

http://y2u.be/M7Flvfx5J10

BIG SPLASH!

Tom Daley has something he wants to say...

Tom Daley was Britain's 2012 Olympic pin-up boy. As the photogenic teenager high-dived his way to a bronze medal, he was swooned over by millions of young girls (as well as their mums and quite a few guys). It's difficult enough for any sportsperson to admit to a gay relationship, but Tom also had a highly marketable boyband-like status to jeopardize. His YouTube "statement", uploaded in December 2013, was not only brave but touchingly delivered as he demonstrated his pride and conviction in such an upbeat, honest and heartwarming fashion.

http://y2u.be/OJwJnoB9EKw

SOMETHING FISHY

TED illuminates the magic of the deep sea

If you have a few minutes to fill, head for YouTube's fascinating collection of TED Talks. TED stands for Technology, Entertainment and Design, and its mini-lectures by the world's leading thinkers and doers cover these topics as well as science, business, politics and the arts. This one is a favourite – oceanographer David Gallo's entertaining talk and jaw-dropping footage of amazing deep sea creatures, including a shape-shifting cuttlefish, a pair of fighting squid and a mesmerizing gallery of bioluminescent fish that light up the blackest depths of the ocean.

http://y2u.be/YVvn8dpSAt0

WHICH DIRECTION?

Boy band in existentialist thriller?

Why would anyone want to have a poke at One Direction? The talented lads with a penchant for harmonies and wispy hair have built a reputation for their sensitive pop pap. But suddenly online wags Bad Lip Reading have turned the boys into laughing stock, by making them the stars of a new foreign arthouse film, *Shadow Pico*. This faux movie trailer, set to the video for the song "Gotta Be You" — all meaningful looks and heartfelt confrontations — is pure gibberish and absolute comedy gold.

http://y2u.be/MYNJwpHWsBg

BEAM ME UP, SCOTTY

Star Trek encounters planet twerk

As soon as Miley and young-ish Robin foisted their twerk upon a wholly suspecting world, the race was on for the best parody. This fabulous mash-up set a pretty high standard. Yep, Captain Kirk, Uhuru, Checkov et al. have seen some pretty horrific stuff on their viewscreen, but what they're about to see will put all those aliens in the shade, although thankfully we're spared the "where no man has been before" comments. For *Breaking Bad* fans, *Hank and Marie Watch Miley Cyrus at the VMAs* is a highly commended runner-up.

http://y2u.be/k6Lb3kFwJRQ

JUST KIDDING AROUND

Because goats just wanna have fun

"Chèvres en équilibre" might sound like a pretentious arty French film from the 1960s, but it's actually one of the best minutes of footage to be uploaded to YouTube in the last couple of years. It translates as "goats balancing" and is just that. Three young goats climb and attempt to stay on a flexible sheet of metal. It's a fabulous playground ride for the farmyard trio, watched over by their tethered elder who gives them a friendly butt every time they jump or fall off. It's innocent, fun and totally, totally captivating.

http://y2u.be/58-atNakMWw

CUPBOARD LOVE

The little lad who tells it like it is

The things you get forced to do when you're a cute little toddler. Go on – tell the nice man what you said to mummy again. Yeah, OK, if it means I'll get something decent to eat. This little chap came up with one little gem of homespun honesty and you can bet it's going to stay with him for years to come. He's already been "made" to repeat his famous sentence over 100 million times online and probably still enjoys the fame. But just wait until he's 14 and his classmates discover his little party piece...

http://y2u.be/E8aprCNnecU

EPIC BEAUTORIAL FAIL

It's enough to make your hair curl

This hilarious two-minute video combines two of YouTube's duller obsessions to create one crazy viral. The number of "epic fail" videos featuring slipping, tripping, blundering idiots is matched only by the volume of beauty tutorials posted by spotty teenagers who have learned to wield an eye pencil. So, step forward Tori Locklear to demonstrate both fads at once. Earnest Tori is itching to bring a little more glamour to the world with an online lesson on how to use a hair-curling iron. Now, let me get this right, I've wrapped my hair in the iron... I've counted to 20... oh-my-god!

http://y2u.be/LdVuSvZOqXM

BUZZ LIKES BIG BUTTS

"Baby Got Back" as sung by the movies

YouTuber dondrapersayswhat describes his video pretty simply.

"Clips from 295 movies used to recreate Sir Mix-A-Lot's 'Baby Got Back' — because I'm just that much of a nerd." Whatever inspired him to use the 1992 hit, which begins, "I like big butts and I cannot lie," isn't made clear, but the musical mash-up is genius, featuring everyone from Buzz Lightyear to Humphrey Bogart and Fred Flintstone to Arnold Schwarzenegger. If you want to play the game and guess the movies, click the caption button at the bottom right of the screen to hide or reveal the titles.

http://y2u.be/wPcap05ZB_o

Muppetational *Oceans 11* movie mash-up

This is a fun game. Take two films that have nothing in common and, with a little editing and redubbing of voices, create a trailer for a brand new movie. A kids' movie can become a horror nightmare or a rom-com can turn into a tense thriller. Sometimes it works spectacularly well and sometimes, well, it looks like two films spliced together. This one cleverly puts together the voices of *Oceans 11* and scenes from *The Muppets*, but you could also check out *Ninja Turtles/Reservoir Dogs*, *You Got Served/Wizard of Oz* or the fabulously titled *Brokeback to the Future*.

http://y2u.be/01Q7I-fPxcM

SIR DOSSER, DJANGO AND THE ACTRESS

Legendary Mila Kunis interview with rookie reporter

It was BBC reporter Chris Stark's big break – an interview with Hollywood star Mila Kunis. The actress was meant to be promoting her new movie, *Oz the Great and Powerful*, but a mixture of bravado, nerves and a star clearly keen to take him off-piste led to the most down-to-earth interview ever. From his opening question – "Did you enjoy being ugly for once? Because, generally, like, you know, you're hot" – to asking her to be his plus-one at his mate Dicko's wedding, the whole thing is funny, charming and has given both their careers a deserved boost.

http://y2u.be/z4Ezruu1oeQ

BOO!

How to scare your boss – and keep your job

Ah! The simple ones are the best. An empty box and a big scream is all you need. We're watching an empty booze warehouse as one guy quietly goes about his work, "Bohemian Rhapsody" playing on the radio in the background. But what happened next caused this clip to be voted best video of the year on Jimmy Kimmel's hit US show. Look for the face pulled by Paul, the boss – that was the clincher for them. Just a word of warning for younger viewers, though: not all bosses are such good sports, so best leave the pranks to the professionals.

http://y2u.be/Uu80TPja2OY

APOCALYPSE AAAAAAAAAAHH!

The job interview at the end of the world

It's a job interview and you know you should be giving your prospective boss your full attention, but you spot something out of the corner of your eye that distracts you, someone rummaging through the drawers in the corner perhaps, a strange photograph or maybe a stray nostril hair. But what if the distraction was the actual end of the world? At what point do you draw your interviewer's attention to this? That's the premise for this well-enacted prank set up by LG to show off its high-definition TV screens.

http://y2u.be/Cer8l4cX-vs

YOUR NEW BEST FRIEND

The ultimate dog tease

Is Andrew Grantham a cruel heartless monster whose idea of fun is to drive his poor dog Clyde to distraction? After all, in separate videos – this one and *Dog Wants a Kitty* – we find him repeatedly goading Clyde into a frenzy of expectation before pitilessly letting him down. The answer is no, Andrew is actually a clever Canadian voice-over comedian whose talking dog videos are brilliantly timed, expertly voiced and, it has to be said, perfectly acted by Clyde. These videos certainly reach out to a certain audience. They each have millions of hits – and only a thousand or so are mine.

http://y2u.be/nGeKSiCQkPw

LITTLE DRUMMER BOY

Time to wake the back-seat drummer

It's great when your toddler falls asleep in the car. You get a rare minute to yourself or a chance to chat to your partner without an interruption every 20 seconds. But there is also a downside. When the kid wakes up, he or she is almost always whiney, grumpy and cranky. But these parents have found the perfect solution to that waking problem. Yep, they start blasting Nirvana's "Breed" from the car stereo and before he's even opened his eyes properly, the little rocker is air drumming like some sad 20-something stoner. Magic.

http://y2u.be/oRm8RmNGFq4

ANTARCTIC ROLL

Penguins doing what they do best – falling over!

They call these guys "nature's comedians". The Antarctic might be cold but it must be one hell of a place for laughs with so many penguins shuffling around. We may not be able to get into their stand-up comedy clubs or laugh along with their sitcoms, but we do get to watch the little fellas falling over, again and again. And, you can't deny they make you laugh – their miniature evening dress colouring, that cute little waddle and the unfortunate fact that these unstable creatures have to walk around on ice. Move over, Monty Python!

http://y2u.be/Tcx6YyXvvRI

SOCKS ROCKS!

Shetland pony dances his way to fame

Phone network Three are pretty keen on their online ads and had a 2014 hit with "Sing it Kitty" (the girl riding on the bike with a kitten in the basket). But Socks, the moonwalking Shetland pony, captured everyone's hearts in their most successful effort. Socks' dance track of choice was Fleetwood Mac's "Everywhere", but it was the blond-maned pony's nifty hoofwork that really caught the eye. He even made a comeback, wearing a Christmas sweater, for a festive campaign. Quite what it had to do with a mobile phone was anyone's guess, but frankly, who cares?

http://y2u.be/Ekr05T9Iaio

TURNING ON THE TAP

"Cups" — the hit tap-dancing version

Tap dancing? Isn't that only done by eight-year-old girls? Hasn't it gone the way of telephone boxes, ventriloquists and sets of *Encyclopaedia Britannica*? Well, no, apparently not, as it's alive and kicking, and these guys are the ones making sure tap dancing is trending. Anna Kendrick's massive hit "Cups (When I'm Gone)" inspired countless YouTube covers, but Christopher Rice and his fellow Broadway dancers clacking and clicking their way through the song is head, shoulders, knees and toes above them all — skilful, subtle, elegant, energetic and, well, pretty damn cool.

http://y2u.be/Q4FYNF02yEM

HITCH-A-RIDE HERO

Just about the strangest news report ever

This clip comes from a local TV news channel in Fresno,
California, and tells how a man claiming to be Jesus drove his
car into a roadside worker and then attacked a female bystander.
So far, so newsworthy. But wait. A homeless hitchhiker, who had
also been in the car, turned out to be the hero of the hour, saving
the woman by attacking the driver with a small axe he happened
to be carrying(!). Now, you must admit, it's getting strange, but
that's not the half of it. Wait until you hear Kai the Hitchhiker
retell the story (with adult language). Mind-blowing!

http://y2u.be/-Xa0NfCdLk4

GRANNY THEFT AUTO

Underage joyrider

"No videos games for an entire weekend." That's what Latarian Milton, a boy from South Florida, thinks his punishment should be for totalling his granny's car. Milton and his buddy wanted to do "hood rat stuff" (as you do), so he took his grandma's Dodge Durango for a ride around the neighbourhood. He hit a couple of cars in a car park and managed to write off the SUV, but what really caught the police's attention was that he couldn't see over the steering wheel. Latarian, you see, is only seven years old!

http://y2u.be/qcqOgnQyXp4

BOXING CLEVER

How much fun can a cat have with a box?

It seems the answer is hours and hours of boundless enjoyment.
For us the question is: how long can we watch a cat having fun
with a box? If this video is anything to go by, it's pretty easy to fill
a good 90 seconds. For this is Maru, a 5.5kg (12lb) Scottish Fold
from Japan, who is fast becoming the Internet's favourite feline.
Maru's working hard for the fame as he has now appeared
in around 200 YouTube videos, mainly jumping in and out of
boxes, but, hey, if you've got a talent, why not milk it?

http://y2u.be/hPzNI6NKAG0

BRING HOME THE BACON

The remarkable Illinois state fair hog-calling contest

This is brilliant. And possibly useful. Because you never know when you might need to know exactly how to call a pig. He could be right over the other side of the field and he's not going to come if you just stand around shouting, "Hey, fatso, come over here." Oh no. These are professional callers with any number of tricks up their snouts, so sit back and prepare to go hog-wild for a hilarious feast of screams, shouts, whines, guttural emissions, snorts and a surprising number of "Here Piggy, Piggy!" calls.

http://y2u.be/uVcVSEa_Ooo

SHOUT AND FALL

Blink and you'll miss it

This one is for all those with short attention spans. Still with us?
OK. See if you can hang in there till the end, although it does
last a whole three seconds, so best bring a snack and a drink
to keep you going. It's worth staying with it, though, because it
could be the funniest three seconds on the net. And, of course,
if you are the kind of person who can't stop laughing at someone
falling over, some kind soul has compiled a feature length
version in *Go Bwah 10 Minute Repeat*.

http://y2u.be/MXgnIP4rMol

MARTIAL ART FAIL

That'll be the universally feared, falling painfully move, then

---

Mark Hicks is a highly trained martial artist, stuntman and actor. In one of YouTube's most famous clips, this video shows his audition for a LeBron James Nike commercial. Hicks prepares to perform his well-practised routine involving a back flip followed by a display of his nunchuck skills. The cameras begin to roll. Play video... hang on, you'll probably need to see that again — and again. A great postscript is that despite the epic fail being leaked to YouTube, Mark was given another chance to demonstrate his skills and actually got the part.

http://y2u.be/BEtloGQxqQs

OH, THE HUGE MANATEE!

When you just can't stop...

Why don't we see more manatees on our screens? These sea cows are calming, mesmerizing and have adorable, funny faces. Just because they don't enjoy savaging other creatures in bloodthirsty attacks, they hardly ever get an up-close documentary on the Discovery Channel. One of them did, however, get a breakthrough viral appearance in a clip that is guaranteed to raise a smile. So, full marks to producer Jordan Mencel for masterfully using Flux Pavilion's massive hit "I Can't Stop" as the perfect soundtrack and transforming an amusing 10-second film into a now legendary YouTube gem.

http://y2u.be/CLGJ-LVCQrM

ARMED ROBBERY RAP

One day all news interviews will be in song

Songify is a simple app that can turn speech into song. It's cheap and easy, so everybody's doing it, but it takes genius to do it with flair. Step forward the Gregory Brothers (under the YouTube username schmoyoho). The original footage was amusing enough — a slightly eccentric eye-witness account of an attempted armed robbery at a petrol station — but put to song it knocks most composed hits into a swag bag. And the lyrics are pretty smart too: "Cos my daddy taught me good" could have come from the lips of Beyoncé.

http://y2u.be/qloG4PIEPtY

FOOD FOR THOUGHT

Help yourself to a bowl of *Western Spaghetti*

Mmm! A delicious bowl of spaghetti with tomato sauce. You'll be licking your lips at the sight of this dish prepared by talented stop-motion artist Pes. But don't kid yourself you'll be able to re-create it at home. This is a cookery demonstration with a difference, as our chef makes use of the most incredible ingredients, including Rubik's Cube garlic, pick-up sticks spaghetti, Post-it note butter. And just wait to see what he uses for pepper. It's a feast for the imagination, if not exactly the stomach, and if this leaves you hungry for more, order up some of Pes' Oscar-nominated *Fresh Guacamole*.

http://y2u.be/qBjLW5_dGAM

ICE CREAM, YOU SCREAM

We all scream for coneing

Ing-ing is a popular pastime on YouTube. We've had planking (lying down), owling (perching) and batmanning (hanging upside down), but it's quite a feat to make up your own "ing" and see it take off across the net. Australian Albi Stevens managed just that. Albi's fast food videos are loved by millions as he befuddles, infuriates and occasionally amuses fast food drive-thru attendants with his pranks. But it is his coneing – grabbing the ice cream by the soft cream and not the cone – that really took off. Even Justin Bieber has posted his own cone-ing video!

http://y2u.be/nn1vMhsePOg

DESTRUCTION CYCLE

Hang on – I've left a sock in there

Russian anarchist Mikhail Bakunin wrote, "The lust of destruction is also a creative lust." He'd have loved this video, if he hadn't been dead for nearly 150 years. After all, at some level we all like smashing something up for the sheer fun of it (don't you?) and Aussie50, producer of this epic five minutes, certainly does. Having taken out the concrete counterweight and put a few hefty objects in for a good wash, Aussie50 then selects what he refers to as the "kill cycle". What happens next is pretty impressive. Just don't try it with your mum's new Zanussi.

http://y2u.be/6_PLnInsh7E

SKIP TO THE GOOD BIT

Skipping – from the rope's point of view

You probably realize by now that YouTube is not the only video-sharing website in town; Vimeo, Vine and others increasingly have their own fans. However, if there's anything excellent posted on one of them, it will likely pop up on the others. Take this fantastic video from Callum Cooper. A fashion film for clothing company Klezinski, it was originally posted on Vimeo. Hypnotic, mesmerizing, beautifully filmed (if slightly nausea-inducing in a rollercoaster kind of way), it takes a unique perspective on a gentle rope-jumping game. Fabulously edited with a great soundtrack, it'll leave you in a spin.

http://y2u.be/x1G2QrasPRk

GIANT GUITARS OR SMALL CHILDREN?

Bizarre footage of North Korean child guitarists

North Korea is one of the world's most secretive states. Very little escapes across its closed borders, but this video was somehow smuggled out. What does it reveal about the North Koreans? That they are unable to manufacture child-sized guitars? That their hairdressing skills lag behind those of the West? Or that they're ready to invade the rest of the world if we ever unleash Jedward upon them? "Creepy as hell" reads the subtitle for the video. That's as maybe, but these kids can't half play a mean guitar!

http://y2u.be/gSedE5sU3uc

GAME OVER

Shooting from the hipster of YouTube

This one is for the dudes who like games such as *Halo* or *Call of Duty* – adventures played out through the eyes of the gamer. Although these games are, of course, incredibly realistic, filmmaker and visual effects wizard Freddie Wong has taken it one big step further. Freddie is a YouTube legend with many viral gaming-based hits under his belt, but this is his most popular effort yet – a kind of scary, kind of funny, vision of a future game in which reality and fantasy are totally blurred.

http://y2u.be/CyCyzBOCedM

EXTRACTION DISTRACTION

Now we know why they're called wisdom teeth

Having your wisdom teeth out — a painful experience for some but a goldmine for those wanting entertaining videos. Pulling fabulous faces with their swollen cheeks, trying to communicate though still groggy from the anaesthetic and seemingly living in a strange parallel world, these post dental-trauma sufferers are earnest and befuddled — and a real hoot. Just watch Julie as she struggles with issues of time travel and tries to solve the case of the missing hat. And when the laughing gas starts to wear off, try *I'm a Nascar Driver or Unicorn After Wisdom Teeth*.

http://y2u.be/zgB2ziyAteI

THE WORLD AT HIS FEET

Remarkable footage of five-year-old Lionel Messi

Remember that boy who could run rings around everyone at playtime football? He was the star of the school team and was even invited to the local club for trials? He's now working in the estate agents in the high street nursing a dodgy knee. But for the little lad slipping through the toddler opposition in this film, the future panned out just the way it looked like it would, because 20 years later Lionel Messi would be the best footballer in the world.

http://y2u.be/Dc8azekvE_s

YOU TALKIN' 'BOUT ME?

The name is the game in a hilarious conference prank

Now it's time for some good, old-fashioned, juvenile fun. There are always some laughs to be had at those big conventions where everyone is forced to wear a name badge, and American comedian Jack Vale totally nails it at the National Association of Music Merchants (NAMM) conference. He's got a good plan and he executes it well, so it's a sure-fire winner. After all, what would you do if you walked past a complete stranger who's talking about you on the phone? Gratifyingly simple and gloriously silly.

http://y2u.be/6w3QmqqCmk0

THE CAT THAT GOT THE CREAM

The Internet phenomenon that is Simon's Cat

___

You've probably come across Simon's Cat already, maybe in a book or a newspaper cartoon strip, but if you haven't seen his YouTube films you're in for a real treat. Creator Simon Tofield's very short, simple, but quirky animations of his mischievous, but endearing, mog (actually based on all three of his own cats) all garner millions of views. There are nearly 50 videos featuring the adventures of the ever-hungry cat. *Let Me In* is a classic episode, which will have you scratching at the door desperate for more.

http://y2u.be/EKvNqe8cKU4

CRASH COURSE

Tribute to the daddy of the monster trucks

Monster trucks are five tons of big, big, noisy fun. OK, they're in real races, but what the punters want to see is these behemoths smashing and crashing their way around a circuit. The Grave Digger is the Godzilla of them – a green and black car crusher with menacing red headlights, it never disappoints. With a blatant disregard for the rules of the road and safety in general (do they even have wing mirrors?), these poster boys of the monster truck world indulge in wild stunts and rollover crashes, and still win the race!

http://y2u.be/WwjGo3kQgMw

ON HIS TROLLEY

Taking a luxury ride

Next time you visit your local supermarket and wonder what's happened to all the trolleys, here's your answer. The local pooches are using them as mobility carts. Watch here as Maymo, the lemon beagle, pushes his puppy sister Penny through the town to the playground. All very cute, but it raises some serious questions. Where would a dog get the token or coin to release the trolley in the first place? Couldn't they do something more useful, like get the weekly shopping? And who is carrying the little plastic bags for their "gifts"?

http://y2u.be/cVg2QEYtdlM

DON'T LOSE YOUR HEAD

The wonderful world of exploding princesses

Simone Rovellini is a bit of a scamp. A digital artist, he excels in "doctoring" well-known films for comic effect. To be honest, Simone is a bit of a one-trick pony, but hey, it's a pretty good trick – he makes your favourite characters' heads explode! His morbidly hilarious video *Exploding Actresses* saw the likes of Julie Andrews, Judy Garland and Ingrid Bergman get the treatment. They were all fair game but this time he's surely taken it too far. Snow White? Cinderella? The Little Exploding Mermaid? Come on, Simone, have a heart!

http://y2u.be/i6cb0ggl8bQ

CHRISTMAS RAPPING

Sick bucket ready – it's a family Christmas video

We've all received those sickeningly smug Christmas cards that, rather than simply saying "Happy Holidays", proceed to fill you in on everything the family has done over the year, from little Archie learning to ride a bike to Mum burning the cupcakes. Well, things have just got worse – people have started to do video versions.

To be fair, the Holderness family's effort is as smart as their Christmas pyjamas as they rap about everything from four-year-old Penn Charles' school recital to six-year-old Lola's ability to count to 100 in Chinese... to Dad's recent vasectomy.

http://y2u.be/2kjoUjOHjPl

A REAL CRY BABY

A mother's song is all too emotional

This 10-month-old's response to her mother's performance of Rod Stewart's "My Heart Can't Tell You No" has brought tears to the eyes of thousands of YouTube viewers. If you want to see the strength of the bond between a mother and her child, just watch baby Mary-Ann's face as she listens to the delightful recital. The way she experiences the emotion of the song is incredibly moving and as the tears well up in her eyes... hold on there, can someone pass me a tissue...

http://y2u.be/nIsCs9_-LP8

UNDERCOVER VIRTUOSO

World famous musician takes to the subway

Here's a question for you: if Beyoncé was singing on a street corner, how long would it take for her to draw a crowd? If Justin Bieber set about busking, how quickly would he fill his cap with loose change. Pretty quickly, yeah? So how about if one of the world's most famous musicians began to play at a busy rail station? The *Washington Post* set up an experiment to find out, persuading violin virtuoso Joshua Bell to flex his much-revered elbow at a Washington DC subway station. What happened next? Take a look...

http://y2u.be/hnOPu0_YWhw

BEDTIME FOR YAUN ZAI

Panda mum deals with the universal parenting problem

In the panda enclosure at Taiwan's Taipei Zoo, Yuan Yuan
is trying to get her youngster Yuan Zai to sleep.
"Come on now, bedtime."
"Oh Mum! Just 10 more minutes? Please."
"Bed!"
"Can I have a drink of water?"
"Nope. You're coming with me."
"Mum, I'm not even tired."
"When I say bed I mean bed. You need your sleep.
Just look at those rings around your eyes!"

http://y2u.be/eRP3h2Lt6wQ

WHAT WERE YOU THINKING?

Barista sends girl his best "seduction" video message

Brody Ryan really thought he was in with a chance. This gorgeous girl had given the barista her number after they'd met at Starbucks. So, in a bid to impress, our wannabe Don Juan sent her a 16-second clip of himself with Drake's "Hold On We're Going Home" playing in the background... uh-oh. She passes the video to a friend who posts it online. Within days there are hundreds of views and in no time at all the *Starbucks Drake Hands* parodies begin... and from Gremlins to Toddlers to Boston Terriers, they're all pretty good.

http://y2u.be/4ki-5_BD7ZwThe

THE DOMINO EFFECT

The greatest falling domino chain ever

If you've ever tried to set up one of those falling domino chains, you'll know just how difficult it is. You spend ages placing them in exactly the right position and the dog walks over them or you sit back, admire your handiwork, topple the first domino, watch six more fall and then the whole thing comes to a frustrating halt. So, little surprise that it took three months for Hevesh5 and Millionendollarboy to set up more than 20,000 dominoes for these amazing tricks — and just minutes to knock them all down.

http://y2u.be/ARM42-eorzE

KILL BILL BABY

Soft toy no match for infant assassin

This thrilling trailer, an homage to both Quentin Tarantino's *Kill Bill* series and *Enter the Dragon*, features the latest in martial art stars, Romeo Elvis Bulte Boivin. He's got the Bruce Lee moves, the Chuck Norris toughness, the Jackie Chan suppleness and he's a cute as a button – because Romeo is only a year old. So when a plushie dragon enters the arena (or back garden, as it is here) he's definitely no match for the soft toy killer, who is all set to knock the stuffing out of him – quite literally.

http://y2u.be/1oHWvFrpocY

WATCH MY LIPS!

What the trombone saw...

And now for something completely different... David Finlayson, the second trombonist in the New York Philharmonic, decided to record an instrument's-eye view of his performance by attaching a camera to his trombone slide. The result is probably quite interesting to musicians and academics, but definitely very amusing to the rest of us. And, if not for his recital, Mr Finlayson certainly deserves a standing ovation for refusing to carry irritating ads on his clip, despite the opportunity to make a few bucks from his most entertaining experiment. Bravo David, bravo!

http://y2u.be/soDn2puEuL8

PUPPET SHOW AND TELL

When kids' TV goes feral

Freaky, freaky, freaky. Is this an attempt at a children's TV puppet show or something much darker? What begins as a friendly educational guide to creativity seems to turn into something very different. It's led to a fair amount of Internet discussion on the meaning of the video — often centring on how children are conditioned to think in certain ways by patronizing TV and videos like these. Both amusing and unsettling, it's a fascinating piece. And maybe you can work out just why green isn't a creative colour.

http://y2u.be/9C_HReR_McQ

BATHTIME FOR KITTY

Cats and the wet stuff – what's not to like?

Just who is the most popular YouTube personality? Bieber, PSY, Miley? Maybe, but they all look jealously at the view count racked up by the domestic cat. Yep, kitty steals the show every time. This video explores that love/hate (OK, mostly hate) relationship between cats and water. Baths, sinks, taps, rivers and swimming pools – they do seem to bring out the playful, the weird, the cute and the downright funny in our furry friends. So by the time you read this, this video will have clocked up around 100 million views – Miley's got to go some to match that!

http://y2u.be/TVvcdQFFYhk

LIKE SCIENCE CLASS – BUT FUN

Put a little Vsauce on your web

Michael Stevens' Vsauce channel almost single-handedly prevents YouTube being classed as a moronic collection of people falling over, showing off or appearing in dubious music videos. Vsauce is a collection of bite-sized videos that reflect a "hyper-curiosity about the world." The short films on science, technology, nature and much more are arranged in various segments, including Mindblow (inventions), FAK (facts and knowledge trivia) and WAC (weird awesome crazy activities from around the world). Charming, engaging and amusing, Stevens is like your favourite-ever science teacher and his lessons only ever last around five minutes!

http://y2u.be/jHbyQ_AQP8c

THE TIPPING POINT

A $200 tip – that must be some service!

How much do you tip for really good service at your local restaurant? 10 percent? Maybe 15 percent if you're in a good mood or even 20 percent if the waiter or waitress is cute. They get a small bonus to the measly wage they are paid and you get a nice smile and leave feeling like you are a pretty decent stand-up guy. But this crowd decided to take the whole tipping scenario even further. They decided to leave $200 tips for waiting staff earning not much more than two dollars an hour – then film their reactions. Perhaps it's no surprise to discover they are pretty pleased...

http://y2u.be/Q4enUE8qt_Q

ELASTIC MAN

Stretchiest skin world record demonstration

The *Guinness World Records* annals are always worth peeking into for entertaining freaks. Here Garry Turner, who's able to pull the skin of his stomach out nearly 16cm (6¼in), shows what he's made of. Some skill, you may think. He must have worked hard at that. However, to Garry it all comes easily. He suffers from a rare medical condition called Ehlers-Danlos Syndrome. Just think — once upon a time, you had to go to a circus to be freaked out. Now you can squirm at the touch of a button.

http://y2u.be/f46SpiboAew

GANDALF ON ACID

Classic old-man-invades-interview clip

It's one of the iconic YouTube videos. This 30-second clip in which an old bloke encroaches on a TV interview has been viewed by millions of people. And you can bet most of them had at least a little chuckle. The ol' fella from the city of Rethymnon, Crete, who has been nicknamed "Greek Grandpa" and "Gandalf on Acid", put in one of the great comedy performances of our time and was rewarded with his own five minutes of fame.

http://y2u.be/iheOMq8UkN4

CUTEST DOG ON THE PLANET

Meet Boo the dog — he's too cute!

"My name is Boo. I am a dog. Life is good" is how this Pomeranian launched his journey to fame. He is now an Internet sensation with 10 million Facebook "likes", his own publications, a job as Virgin America's "spokesdog" and an endorsement by Khloe Kardashian, who says he is indeed the "cutest dog on the planet." So here's your chance to see what all the fuss is about. Boo being shy, Boo dressed up, Boo playing with a soft toy. It's nothing any old mongrel hound couldn't do, but there's no denying it, this dog is darned cute.

http://y2u.be/peKSCssJTqE

FLIPPING BRILLIANT!

Cristiano Ronaldo comes to life in a flipbook

Etoilec1 is a bit of a mystery figure. No one seems to know much about him, except he can certainly draw! He has done some impressive manga-type flip books and a great "Gangnam Style" book, but he is really inspired when it comes to drawing footballers. He's paid flip-book homage to Ronaldinho, Zlatan Ibrahimovic and Lionel Messi, but it's the extravagant skills of the Portuguese prodigy Cristiano Ronaldo that really come to life on his pages. And not a theatric tumble in sight!

http://y2u.be/B_C79HadggE

TRAFFIC JAM

White Van Man sings the blues

White Van Man has a bad reputation. The drivers and passengers of these utility vehicles are often seen as sexist, angry and belligerent. These two guys might have been actors paid by the White Van Man publicity department to improve their image. But they're not. They're just two working blokes on the way to a job, having a laugh as their favourite tune blasts from the van's speakers. It's a hoot!

http://y2u.be/urPq6PVa3-o

YOUTUBE BY POST

Enjoy YouTube offline

Spare a thought for those people who find the Internet daunting and unreliable. How do you find what you want? How do you know someone's not watching you through your computer or tablet? And where do all these videos come from? In 2012 those thoughtful people at YouTube took note of these concerns and announced this amazing service — all of YouTube on DVD delivered to your door! No more worries about download capacity or streaming capabilities. Just pop a disk into your player.
Note: this video was posted on 1 April...

http://y2u.be/Y_UmWdcTrrc

SMALL GIRL, BIG BIRD, PONY

An epic encounter

Here's a nice little clip of a small girl taking her first ride on her pony. She trots around in a field quite happily, but then a long-legged bird monster appears and things go all Pete Tong – in the most hilarious way. So who will win? The pony and the toddler or the adult ostrich? Who's your money on? Do keep watching to the end, though. The pony does a fabulous "nothing to do with me" exit.

http://y2u.be/AlO0x2gAnvM

SILENT ERA CELL PHONE

Time traveller spotted in Charlie Chaplin film

People today, eh? They can't do anything without taking their phone along and yapping continuously. You'd think if you managed to time travel back to the 1920s you'd have something better to do than call your friend to discuss who said what to whom. But consider this bystander found on the extras on the DVD of Charlie Chaplin's 1928 film *The Circus*. She really does seem to be chatting on her phone. Explain that one, then!

http://y2u.be/TiIrpEMbQ2M

DUNKIN' DOBBIN

Horse tries out new jumping technique

Compared with humans, animals always manage to look so graceful and co-ordinated. You never see them walking into lampposts, tripping over their own feet or taking the stairs seven at a time. Take the horse, for example — serene when still, graceful at a trot and powerful at full speed. You would never get a thoroughbred making a complete ass of himself, would you? Well, somehow this nag manages to prove the exception. Memorize his face and remember not to back him in a steeplechase.

http://y2u.be/YBkmefllgiE

DEMON DOG

Staines gets psyched by cupcakes

Anyone who's seen the iconic *Dramatic Chipmunk* YouTube clip will know where this one is heading. It features Staines, an Australian Shepherd dog, who is appearing on a TV dog-training show. For the discipline test, the dog is presented with a plateful of cupcakes and must retain its self-control. As the strain begins to show it seems that the only way Staines will get through it is to enter a zen-like trance...

http://y2u.be/t-XIMEHGoZI

DAD DENIAL DANCE

Andrew and his famous "not the father" moves

You may have seen this in the background of the hit movie *Bridesmaids*, but it's worth a giggle or two in its own right. This is a segment from US TV's *The Maury Povich Show* on US TV, where private domestic disputes are aired in public. Now, for many men, the moment they discover they're a father is one they treasure for life. But not Andrew. He's been told by the child's mother that she's 5,000 percent sure she's had his baby, but he's holding out for the DNA test to prove otherwise. Will he be proud as punch or quietly relieved? Oh no...

http://y2u.be/vt2i0ts-uck

GONE WITH THE WIND

Hurricane "Bawbag" rolls into town

Mother Nature has a pretty good sense of humour at times. Here, she's whipped up a rare old storm in Cowdenbeath, Scotland, with gusts reaching up to 265km/h (165mph). Although such winds are often destructive, ruining people's houses and lives, in this particular case old Mrs N has just decided to have a laugh. Fortunately, local resident Conor Guichan was filming the hurricane through his window at the time – and manages to provide the perfect commentary as an unusual object sweeps past his window...

http://y2u.be/UPKb9z4I7eM

MASHED UP WITH KETCHUP

Ketchup robot with epic soundtrack

Looking for a good-value video? Then check this out: two
YouTube classics for the price of one. Firstly, you get to watch
the almost amazing *Ketchupbot*. Actually called the Automata,
it's an invention straight from the world of Wallace and Gromit,
because a robot ketchup dispenser would be absolutely awesome
if, well, it worked. But never fear, for the soundtrack is YouTube's
infamous *20th Century Fox Fanfare Played on Flute* (in fact,
a recorder), a travesty so perfectly executed that it
fits the video like a glove.

http://y2u.be/4WX58CZwyiU

128

MARRY ME, LIVE

After this, the wedding had better be good...

OK, you'll either love this or really hate it. Perhaps the latter if you don't consider it romantic to share your marriage proposal with anyone who has an Internet connection or if your idea of spontaneity doesn't involve roping in every long-lost relation, friend and passing acquaintance and spending hours in rehearsal. However... the resulting video has been enjoyed by over 25 million viewers and even the most cynical of us might have to admit to a lump in the throat when Isaac finally pops the question. It would be even funnier if she said "no", though!

http://y2u.be/5_v7QrlW0zY

KING OF THE SWINGERS

It's the largest rope swing in the world!

When these guys built a rope swing, they didn't just chuck a rope over the nearest branch. They made the largest rope swing in the world. Their carefully constructed rig was built over a natural sandstone structure called Corona Arch in Moab, Utah, USA. It had a pendulum 75m (250ft) long and a drop of 45m (150ft) before the rope even got taut. But this was no child's play. If the set-up went wrong, there would be serious consequences. After it went viral, adrenaline-fuelled daredevils flocked to ride the arch, until a tragic accident led to the authorities drastically restricting its use.

http://y2u.be/4B36Lr0Unp4

KITTY GRINDING THE CRACK

Introducing the world's first BASE jumping cat

If you've watched the BASE jumper Jeb Corliss video *Grinding the Crack*, you will understand the joke here – it's even cut to the same music. If YouTube has done anything, it has proved that cats aren't always cool, they don't always land on their feet and they are as capable as looking as clumsy as a drunk in a supermarket. This cat does its utmost to be catlike. Inscrutable and thoughtful, it clearly has a plan, but it's not going to be rushed into action. Watch as it sizes up the situation, assesses the task and only then does it jump...

http://y2u.be/Veg63B8ofnQ

COMPLETELY BARKING

Weird dog with an even weirder bark

This is the dog's chops – a fantastic gabbling poodle-cross that
sounds as weird as it looks. You might be tempted to wonder just
what it's talking about, but I really wouldn't bother. If you did
manage to translate the strange yelpings, they'd probably be the
equivalent of that strange bloke at the bus stop screaming, "The
cucumbers are coming to get us. Guard your rawlplugs!" But if
you enjoy this – and you will – be sure to check out *Videoresponse
to The Weirdest Dog Ever*, then explain what that's all about!

http://y2u.be/lvD8WcrdK5o

RETURN OF THE SINGING SPACEMAN

Space station star Chris Hadfield is back on the radar

Chris Hadfield's amazing film of his cover of David Bowie's "Space Oddity" recorded at the International Space Station was one of the most talked about YouTube videos ever. But there's more to the Commander than a good voice. In fact, he's made a fascinating array of videos of life in space, from *How to Wash Your Hand in Space* to *How to Make a Sandwich in Space*. But the Canadian astronaut has also furthered his recording career with ISS (Is Someone Singing/International Space Station), a duet in which Chris performs his part in space, while Barenaked Ladies' frontman Ed Robertson sings along in downtown Toronto.

http://y2u.be/AvAnfi8WpVE

A SELFIE-MADE MAN

The selfie is dead. Long live the super-selfie!

It all happened a couple of years ago. Suddenly everyone was taking a selfie – a picture of themselves that said, "Look at me! Aren't I just the most fun guy ever?" When President Obama was seen taking a selfie at Nelson Mandela's funeral it seemed the whole world had gone mad. But wait. Gabriel Valenciano was working on a super-selfie – a series of pictures in which the hyperactive 1980s gym throwback works it to the *Space Jam* soundtrack. In 15 top YouTube seconds, he smashes it with excess energy, enthusiasm and humour. Top effort.

http://y2u.be/Sp9xfM6SSTI

COOL CROW

A brilliant bird who likes to hit the slopes

If you thought snowboarding 10-year olds speeding past you on the slopes was humiliating enough, wait until you see this common garden bird practicing on a board. It isn't actually a bird-sized snowboard, but a lid from a mayonnaise jar, but there's no doubting that he's using it to ride the snow and going back for more. It's quite a recent clip so expect more in the extreme bird sport series, maybe a pigeon on a BMX or a seagull on a surfboard?

http://y2u.be/n7hiuXjXJEw

DANGEROUS DINNER DATE

More animals eating their food

MisterEpicMann and friends took the biscuit for Britain's YouTube video of the year for their imitations of the table manners of various animals. It may not be exactly educational but it certainly caught the imagination of the online community, who contributed many of their own tributes and parodies. Best leave it to the experts, though, so thankfully the original creators have returned with part two, which includes a hawk, a cheetah, a fruit fly (disgusting!) and an octopus. Now you may think it's just slapstick but as you shake your head at the nonsense people watch, I bet you can't suppress a little chuckle here and there.

http://y2u.be/lp2qchPjk-l

HAMBURGER HERO

Cleveland kidnapping rescuer's meaty interview

"I barbeque with this dude. We eat ribs and whatnot!" In helping
to save three women and a girl from dreadful captivity in a
Cleveland cellar, Charles Ramsey became a national hero in the
US. But in giving one of the best TV news interviews ever, the
effusive 43-year-old became an Internet sensation. They should
show this to all novice reporters as an example of how
to add excitement, colour, product endorsement and a
little fun to even the grimmest of stories — even if he
did appear to stretch the facts at times!

http://y2u.be/gcLSl3oyqhs

PING-PONG PADDLE POW!

Awesome table tennis bat knife-flicking stunt

This is a version of ping-pong you won't have seen before. Out of Sweden came this 30-odd second clip showing a guy using table tennis bats to propel knives that an accomplice catches with her own outstretched bats. Pretty amazing, but they then take the whole stunt to an even more extreme level. "Unbelievable!" you cry. And you have a point. Now take a look at the YouTube video *Miss Ping Debunk*. In a few witty and entertaining minutes, Captain Disillusion completely deconstructs the stunt, showing exactly how they faked the extraordinary trick.

http://y2u.be/5NO-fka_JTQ

WHO'S IN CHARGE?

Advice from the little backseat driver

YouTube is full of cute kids saying sweet or clever things, but this one does stand out. It features dad Ryan Hunley as he offers to help August, his young daughter, buckle herself into her car seat. Now August has reached the independent old age of two and doesn't consider she needs her father's meddling anymore. Will she forgive him for posting it when she's older? Well, in a short interview on *"Have You Ever Had a Dream Like This" Kid – 14 Years Later*, the most famous YouTube child ever didn't seem to mind.

http://y2u.be/4A6Bu96ALOw

(NEAR) DEATH OF A SALESMAN

Racing driver takes a test drive like no other

As ads for soft drinks go, this is a super-fizzy prank. Jeff Gordon, the famous American racing car driver, is disguised and "geeked up" before calling on a car dealer. Eager to secure a deal, the salesman encourages him to take a test drive in the speedy Chevy Camaro. However, once behind the wheel, our nervous nerd becomes a little too bold... and if you wonder if the video is real, watch *Test Drive 2*, where Jeff plays another high-speed prank on a car journalist who doubted him in print.

http://y2u.be/Q5mHPo2yDG8

PET SOUNDS

Time for a little cat chat

Talking cats, eh? So what do they talk about? Tales of last night's scrap with next-door's ginger tom? That annoying bloke who kicks them every time his girlfriend leaves the room? Or the science behind that whole length of whisker/width of body equation? If this video is anything to go by, YouTubers Talking Animals seem to have a pretty good idea of feline banter. These two kitties have a neat line in petty arguments and sneaky plans to get treats, all performed with extraordinary realism. Nine out of ten comments agree – it's a winner!

http://y2u.be/1JynBEX_kg8

HARRY POTTERFY'S THE WORLD

More magic from Potter Puppet Pals

It has now been over seven years since Neil Cicierega's magnificent, slightly off-message Harry Potter puppet series went on YouTube. The third episode, *The Mysterious Ticking Noise*, remains in the Top 50 most-viewed videos ever. The puppet characters are very loosely based on the popular series, but while JK Rowling's Harry Potter series has long since come to an end, Potter Puppet Pals continue to produce high-class episodes. This 2013 short – only 53 seconds long – sees the Pals' ever-vain and arrogant Harry finding a solution to everyone's problems, even the viewers'.

http://y2u.be/QM-TT6KTQNw

RED BULL WINGS

Adrenaline-fuelled mountain bike excitement

It's amazing. You can spend hour after hour, day after day,
watching YouTube clips and you'll still come across something
that completely blows you away. This is another video combining
those old favourites – a GoPro camera and extreme sport –
but this is possibly the best yet. New Zealand's Kelly McGarry
is competing at the Red Bull Rampage, a notoriously gnarly
downhill mountain bike competition held in Utah, USA. The
course itself is terrifying, but that's not enough for Kelly,
who tops it by pulling off an incredible backflip over
a 22m (72ft) canyon. He came second...

http://y2u.be/x76VEPXYaI0

FACE TO FACE

Reincarnation enacted in a trippy time-lapse self-portrait

This is the video artwork of British artist Emma Allen, whose self-portrait explores the idea of rebirth and illustrates the transfer of energy from one incarnation to another. In an incredible journey, the model's face is transformed through the ageing process until she resembles a white skull. It's mesmerizing to watch, but what happens next is totally surprising and beautiful. It took Emma five days of face painting and shooting to make all the frames for the animation, and she has been rewarded with a dreamlike 75 seconds that takes its place as a YouTube must-see.

http://y2u.be/07Ch4A9PnZl

DON'T LOSE YOUR MARBLES

The Internet sensation that is Jenna Marbles

According to the *New York Times*, Jenna Marbles is "the woman with one billion clicks". She is the most successful female poster on YouTube and 13 million YouTubers subscribe to her channel, where she offers advice on anything from *How To Trick People Into Thinking You're Good-Looking* to *A Drunk Make-Up Tutorial*. Jenna's operation is distinctly lo-fi — mostly shot in her own apartment using just a single fixed camera. She gets by because she is sassy, likeable and extremely funny. This is a pretty good example of her work, although she does tend to use fruitier language on many of her other videos.

http://y2u.be/dp-AxFdUe4A

MUTT WITH THE MOVES

Nathan, the happy dancing dog

Here's Nathan, whipping his hair back and forth and moving like he was born on the dance floor. Pharrell Williams' hit song "Happy" was everywhere in 2014 and was just crying out for someone to have a viral hit. So step forward, Nathan, possibly the ugliest dog in the world, for a well-earned five minutes of fame. And it couldn't be a lovelier story. Nathan was a rescue dog with quite a sad past, but by the look of things he's settled down pretty well in his new home!

http://y2u.be/x_wgb1q1opQ

KUNG FU GRANDPA

Dead-beat commentary cuts
down nunchucking senior citizen

You know how it is: you head out early in the morning to a empty supermarket car park to practise a few kung fu moves and give your nunchucks a bit of air. Then, by the time you've got home and sat down with a coffee, you discover you're the star of a viral video and, to add insult... they're calling you Kung Fu Grandpa. That's roughly what happened to 52-year-old Tom Bell after a little workout in his local parking lot. And the hilarious commentary? That's courtesy of one Rev. Aamon Miller, a man of the cloth! Who can you trust? A real gem.

http://y2u.be/gYvw68IneV4

OFFICE CHAIR BOOGIE

The original *Numa Numa* guy

Gary Brolsma was one of the first YouTube stars and his *Numa Numa* video has now breached the 50 million-hit mark. The video is just a webcam recording of Gary sitting in his computer chair, infectiously lip-syncing and dancing along to a 2003 song called "Dragostea din Tei" by Moldovan-Romanian boy band, O-Zone. This is YouTube at its best, spreading joy and a little magic, so join those 50 million viewers and go watch it!

http://y2u.be/60og9gwKh1o

WHAT GOES UP...

Vertigo-inducing rock climbing madness

Skip this one if you're scared of heights, but the rest of you are in for a treat, as rock climber Alex Honnold takes on El Sendero Luminoso, a 457m (1,500ft) high wall in Mexico. Alex is a free solo climber, meaning he goes up alone and he doesn't use ropes, harnesses and other protective gear while climbing. There is absolutely no room for error – even the slightest slip-up would be catastrophic. If you can bear to watch to the hair-raising end, you'll find a link to the full six-minute video.

http://y2u.be/wX_rh8Qugt0

BEHIND THE BRICKS

That hilarious *LEGO Movie* trailer

The blockbuster that was *The Lego Movie* probably didn't need a lot of selling, but this featurette trailer is as good as marketing can get. It works so well because, with tongues firmly in cheeks, the characters, voiced by the actors, talk about the actors playing them. Clever, eh? It's a complete hoot — and where else do you get the chance to *actually* hear Morgan Freeman read the telephone directory?

http://y2u.be/cH4tMSd3QJY

THE BOTTOM LINE

Miley's off to twerk

Miley Cyrus can hold her head up with pride. She was great
in *Hannah Montana*, has a quadruple-platinum debut album,
five non-consecutive Number 1 albums in the US and a fine
collection of tattoos. But this is what she will be remembered
for: a raunchy, and it has to be said cringe-making, performance
alongside Robin Thicke at the VMA awards. The debate was
instant — unacceptable behaviour or just a bit of fun? It became
the most tweeted-about event in history and ensured even
the furthest reaches of civilization now know how to "twerk".

http://y2u.be/tMVJMPvQwY4

IT WON'T TAKE A MINUTE

Sound advice in 59 seconds

Throw those diet books away, here's 59 seconds of scientific weight loss advice. Psychologist Richard Wiseman, a former magician with a PhD in the psychology of deception, has a YouTube channel with over a million subscribers and 200 million views. Prof Wiseman believes that tiny alterations in our lives can make a huge difference to our overall happiness. His collection of under-a-minute videos contain simple, science-based, life-changing tips, from *How to Impress in Meetings* to *Cutting Down on Drinking the Easy Way* and intriguing bite-sized tests such as *Are You a Good Liar?*

http://y2u.be/zDGaXoMRLTU

THE SHINY GUY WORRIES

Star Wars explained by a three-year-old

If it's not bad enough that fully grown adults are attending
Star Wars conventions in their droves and dressing up as star
troopers or whatever, now they have resorted to forcing their
children to explain the plot. Shouldn't there be laws about that
kind of cruelty? To be fair, the cute kid in this famous clip does a
pretty good job, nailing various characters, including C-3PO ("the
shiny guy always worries") and Obi-Wan Kenobi ("he sometimes
moves things around"). I know what you're thinking, though.
Any chance of getting her to explain _The Matrix_ trilogy?

http://y2u.be/EBM854BTGL0

UNHAPPILY EVER AFTER

The unfortunate fate of Disney princesses – in song

"And they all lived happy ever after." YouTuber Jon Cozart, aka Paint, takes the ending as the beginning in his Disney parody that went viral with 30 million views and counting. In a self-made, single-handed, barbershop quartet-style song, Paint takes four Disney princesses and explains what happened next. Mermaid Ariel is a victim of sea pollution; Jasmine's worried about Aladdin, who is locked up in Guantanamo; Pocahontas is a renegade killer; and Belle, well, she has a lot of explaining to do. It's witty, original and brilliantly executed – and Paint's *Harry Potter in 90 Seconds* is worth a quick look too.

http://y2u.be/diU70KshcjA

TAKE A TABLET

Incredible iPad painting of Morgan Freeman

If you thought your iPad was useful only for playing Angry Birds and catching up on *Game of Thrones* on your commute home, have a look at what artist Kyle Lambert has been up to on his tablet. Using only a finger, an iPad Air and the app Procreate, we can watch a time-lapse record of his gobsmackingly realistic portrait of actor Morgan Freeman. (It actually took him 200 hours and 285,000 brush strokes to complete.) Of course, some claim it's a hoax but Kyle and the app manufacturers are standing by the astonishing video.

http://y2u.be/uEdRLlqdgA4

WHO YOU LOOKING AT?

The ultimate showdown: animals versus mirrors

Doh! It's a mirror, stupid. Time to feel superior and watch cats, dogs, lizards and birds making fools of themselves in front of... themselves. Whether they're looking to impress, fight, mate or are just curious about their mirror image, they still end up looking pretty silly and, of course, kind of cute. The puppy backing off from its own image is particularly memorable. Yep, this confirms we humans really are the master species. Now let's go back to watching three hours of epic fails and people falling over...

http://y2u.be/kG_QhttG6jo

PUPPY LOVE

Featuring the most patient cat in the world

Another day, another thousand cat videos appear on YouTube. But
does anyone ever consider the workers? The poor moggies
are forced to spend hours in rehearsals and make-up just
to look extra cute in front of the camera, only to be rewarded
with the odd treat or an old cotton reel... big deal.
The National Union of Cats is determined to put an end to
the exploitation. Its members are hard-working and professional,
and deserve more. Just look at the poise and patience of
this kitty – he waited until the camera was turned
off to savage the irritating pooch.

http://y2u.be/WHuaKpimSqg

TRICK IS THE TREAT

The fabulous return of the *Halloween Candy* prank

It's the gift that keeps on giving! For the third successive year, American TV show host Jimmy Kimmel ran his *I Told My Kids I Ate All Their Halloween Candy Challenge* and was rewarded with another five minutes of angry, stomping, crying, howling brats – all distraught that their hard-earned sugar treats had been secretly pigged by their parents. Greedy and unforgiving children, heartless and cruel adults – it doesn't exactly show the human race in its best light, but it is utterly hilarious. And come on, admit it: you, too, half regret the happy ending. If only the parents had actually eaten the sweets...

http://y2u.be/RK-oQfFToVg

OFF THE LINE

Best-ever goal line clearance

It's frustrating enough to see your goal-bound shot get cleared off the line, but when the opposition's last-gasp saviour isn't even one of their team you have a right to be annoyed. That's just what happens as Brazilian Série D club, Tuti, bear down on the goal of their opponents, Aparecidence. The defending team's masseur is the culprit/hero who keeps the game tied at 2–2 and sends Aparecidence through to the semi-finals. Quite whether the Tuti players have stopped chasing him yet hasn't been reported.

http://y2u.be/f8NhAWiYLCE

DEAD GIVEAWAY MAGIC

Stuart shows he's got the Edge on other magicians

There's plenty of great magic on YouTube, but Stuart Edge's one
dollar/thousand dollar note trick has a feel-good factor many
other contenders lack. Stuart (whose *Mistletoe Kissing Prank* is
also quite sweet) selects those in need of a pick-me-up
for his trick and allows them to keep whatever note magically
appears in their hand. As you might imagine,
the participants are genuinely bowled over.

http://y2u.be/7U1fuQF0KjQ

DUN-DUN, DUN-DUN, DUN-DUN, DUN-DUN

Sharks on film

Real-life shark footage can scare your pants off – those sleek
movements, the naked aggression, those very pointy teeth – but
you can also sit through hours of Discovery Channel or YouTube
shark vids and find the moment of attack is all blurred by
a mass of bubbles and a hastily departing diver. However,
shark attacks in the movies deliver clear water, close-ups
and acrobatic sharks with severed limbs in their mouths.
Every detail is perfectly captured. This montage, put
together by the *Huffington Post*, collects the best of
big-screen attacks from *Jaws* to the *Deep Blue Sea*.

http://y2u.be/wnKrWOpUwR0

RUN RABBIT RUN

Sweary commentary on rabbit outrider

First, a warning: there's some pretty bad language bandied about on this video, so if that sort of thing offends, watch it on mute – it'll still make you smile. Now, do you remember that rabbit on the Duracell battery ad that kept running and running? Well, he's back – in real life! This is footage from railway engineer Craig Woods, featuring the voices of his pals, as their van tries to overtake a bunny on a Scottish country road. It's hilariously surreal.

http://y2u.be/wVN4PRLrpsA

BALL CONTROL

A sport that's bubbling under

Back when defenders were as hard as nails and forwards were nervous, football was a man's game. Nowadays, footballers are so pampered they might as well play in their own safe little bubbles. What? They already do? And it turns out to be very, very funny. The players are encased in zorb-like inflatable bubbles and are allowed to bounce into each other as they try to tackle. No one gets hurt and when they roll around like toy-town figures, trying to get back on their feet, it's highly entertaining. This has got to be the future of sport, hasn't it?

http://y2u.be/xll45f6i1PU

HEADBANGING FIREMAKING

Forget the Stone Age, welcome to the Rock Age

Don't worry. You're safe here. No actual rock music can be heard in this video. In fact, that's the real fun of it. All we hear is the soothing sounds of nature. If it wasn't for the Speedos, grungy shorts and T-shirts, this might pass for ancient footage of Neolithic man making fire while worshipping the great hair god. In these days of professional YouTubers, there's something reassuring about unintentionally funny footage still finding its way to a wide audience. This even has a perfect, almost poetic, ending. Rock on, dudes!

http://y2u.be/389DkzjHpus

PUCKER UP

20 strangers meet for a first kiss

It's a great idea: find 10 pairs of total strangers willing – after a short introduction and some small talk – to indulge in a "proper" first kiss. For all that this is an ad (for a clothing company) and the "strangers" are a little too relaxed and good-looking, it is sensitively observed (in black and white), charming and sensual. The kisses, some a little awkward, some more passionate, may call to mind your own first kiss. Or they might make you squirm and start shouting, "For heaven's sake – get a room!"

http://y2u.be/IpbDHxCV29A

MAN'S BEST FRIEND

If people were pets

This very funny film considers who makes for the better human companion – the over-affectionate hound or the indifferent mog? Fatawesome's unique spin is that they ask what life would be like if your mates acted like your pets. How would you cope with someone who greeted you like a long-lost friend when you'd only been out for five minutes? Or how would you feel about your buddy waking you up in the middle of the night because he fancied some cereal? They've also made an amusing sequel showing just how these pet "friends" can really mess up your life.

http://y2u.be/GbycvPwr1Wg

HEY PRESTO! AAAAAHHHH!

Magic trick with spectacular finale

Ah, the old tablecloth trick. Whipping a tablecloth from under a tea set without breaking your mum's best china can be pretty difficult to execute, but, as a magic trick, yawn! It's been done a million times and lacks any pizazz or excitement. However, these lads have got the tablecloth part down toa fine art and solved the problem by adding a finale that's surprising, dramatic and dangerous! Now all you have to work out is whether it's real or faked.

http://y2u.be/i8Nivk_0TkI

THEME PARK TORTURE

The rollercoaster ride he'll never forget

At most theme parks, they now film every single ride the punters take, so for a few notes, you and your friends can buy a souvenir. This is great, because when you get home you can have a real laugh at your gurning and screaming faces in the minutes before your threw up behind the candy floss stall. But there is a more sinister side to this practice. An employee is watching all those videos in the hope of finding a humiliating clip with which to blackmail some poor sap. Here's one who evidently never paid up – now, of course, a YouTube classic.

http://y2u.be/0MD6Cx0qzRA

GET YOU!

Singing policemen camp it up

One of the best moments of the Sochi Winter Olympics Games must have been the Russian Interior Ministry Police singing at the opening ceremony. While the London Olympics featured Paul McCartney, The Who and the Spice Girls, and Beyoncé appears at the opening of an envelope in the US, the Russians decided to humiliate their once-feared secret police by making them perform the campest rendition ever of Daft Punk's "Get Lucky". They make a pretty good fist of it but those interrogation rooms will never seem as intimidating again.

http://y2u.be/pOTt8QZWSdw

DESPOTIC DOODLES

North Korean dictator draws his life

Anyone who is anyone on YouTube is posting a "draw my life". These are a series of stick drawings or scribbled figures on a whiteboard that tell the events of a person's life. YouTube celebs Jenna Marbles and Ryan Higa have both made funny and poignant versions, but somehow Korean dictator Kim Jong-un has got in on the act. His drawings tell of his remarkable birth, his rise to fame, schooldays in "Sweetserland", losing weight and his success with the ladies. YouTube is banned in North Korea, but they have their own version of the Internet, where this might well be repeated endlessly.

http://y2u.be/U_pZNH_ltDU

THE CALL OF THE WILD

Classic animal footage – with added soundtrack

Life in the wild can be a desperate bid for survival. Become too conspicuous and any minute could be your last. That's why animals communicate softly and without undue fuss. Just watch the subtle and understated way that this marmot attempts to contact his friend Alan – or could that be Steve? Meanwhile, in the depths of the ocean, the sharks practise their theme tune, knowing that one bum note could ruin the whole attack! There's plenty of voiced-over animal clips to choose from on YouTube, but this one combines two winners in a 90-second gem.

http://y2u.be/XgvR3y5JCXg

JUMPING TO CONCLUSIONS

Watch out for that bollard!

Parkour is so cool. It treats the urban environment as a natural obstacle course – the city becomes a physical challenge. To perform at the top level demands immense strength, amazing agility, bravery, a daredevil mentality and an up-to-date *A-Z*. Even the French name for the sport sounds cool. So... it's extra fun when these ghetto gymnasts make real idiots of themselves in some of the most painful ways possible – and still try to maintain their dignity. We can reassure you that all of the participants in this hilarious video *were* harmed during the filming.

http://y2u.be/TuXju71wMts

THE ONLY WAY IS ESSEX

Ellen DeGeneres' pint-sized protégées

YouTube has some extraordinary stories but few match the adventure of Sophia Grace Brownlee from Essex. In 2011, her aunt uploaded this video of Sophia Grace singing the Nicki Minaj rap "Super Bass" as her five-year-old cousin Rosie danced along. In two weeks, the video had gained over 40 million views. Soon, Sophia Grace and Rosie were being flown over to the USA to appear with Nicki on Ellen DeGeneres' hit TV show (you can see that on YouTube, too). Wowed by the girls' distinctive English accents and attitude, Ellen ensured they became the most popular (or irritating) English imports since Posh and Becks.

http://y2u.be/ti-IDMPIT_4

A DOGS' DINNER

Join Nono and Sia on a posh dinner date

"Hey, Sia, where are you having dinner tonight?"
"Same as ever – in the corner of the kitchen, right where they keep my bowl."
"Fancy something a little different?"
"Have you been stealing from the bin again, Nono?"
"No. I just thought we might go out."
"This isn't leading up to your Nandogs or McDogalds joke again, is it?"
"No, dawg! Get your best jumper on – we're going upmarket..."

http://y2u.be/EVwIMVYqMu4

MIND THE GAP, YAH

Posh boy Orlando becomes an intern

Posh student Orlando became an Internet celebrity after posting a series of videos of his calls to his friend Tarquin back in Fulham. Like many students, Orlando spent his gap year travelling the world in order to go on the lash and vomit over various third world destinations. Orlando was too good a character for his creator Matt Lacey to lose so, now back from his "gap yah", we find him ringing to tell Tarquin all about his recent internships in "arrrt", the "meedjah" and "Parrr-liament".

http://y2u.be/hLm2wv4r2ss

If you enjoyed this book,
you're sure to love *The Most
Amazing YouTube Videos Ever*,
also available from Carlton Books